My Special Juneteenth Name

By Darlene Green

Published by: Legacy Voice Productions
Printed in the United States of America

Cover & Illustrations by: Fatima Zeeshan
ISBN: 978-1-960179-39-5

To contact author for booking or ordering additional copies, go to: degreen@cox.net

Special Dedication

This book is dedicated to my father, Walter H. Green, Sr. My father was a courageous warrior in the Civil Rights movement. I'm sure that he led a joyful celebration in Heaven when Juneteenth was declared a federal holiday in the United States on June 17, 2021. Thanks, Dad, for volunteering to serve on the battlefield for justice and making our country and the world better places.

Juneteenth Eve Rap

It was the night before Juneteenth, it was Juneteenth Eve!
Everyone was excited about the gifts they were about to receive!
But the greatest gift of all,
It's not going to a party in a great hall.
It's the valuable history lessons we're about to recall.
Our ancestors paved the way,
So that we can celebrate this great day.
So, sit back and relax!
As we learn some valuable history facts!

June Jones lives in Galveston, Texas with her parents. June enjoys spending time with her family and friends and is excited about Mother's Day, which will be next week. June has a special gift for her mother and looks forward to giving it to her.

It is the morning of Mother's Day and June is excited to give her mom her gift. Before they depart for church services, June gives her mother a beautiful jewelry box, with her mother's name inscribed on it: Mrs. Zarielle Jones.

June's mother gives her a big hug, thanks her, and exclaims that it is the best gift that she has ever received!

Mrs. Zarielle Jones

Later, that evening, after they return from church and have dinner, June goes to bed and is feeling sad. June begins to think about the present she gave her mother, with her mom's name, Mrs. Zarielle Jones, on it. June thinks that her mom's name is the most beautiful name in the world and wonders why her mom did not name her Zarielle also. Her friend, Nina, is named after her mother.

I wish my name could be Zarielle.

June falls asleep, while wishing that she had a fairy Godmother, who can grant her 3 wishes and has a wonderful dream. In June's dream, a fairy Godmother appears and tells June that she is there to grant her 3 wishes that will take place very soon and June is very happy to learn this.

June tells her fairy Godmother that her first wish is to be named after her mother and to change her name from June to Zarielle because it is so beautiful. Besides, one time, some mean kids at school teased her because she is named after a month – "June is bursting out all over." But, her teacher, Ms. Green, told the students not to bully her or say mean things and they stopped and never teased her again. June's fairy Godmother explained that she needed to be very careful when making wishes, because they could not be reversed.

June also tells her fairy Godmother that they would be going to the Jones Juneteenth Family Reunion the next month, and she would love to go to this special event with the same name as her mother, Zarielle. June said: "Zairelle can be my special Juneteenth name!" June's fairy Godmother tells her that she loves the holiday, Juneteenth, and that is why she is dressed in her African outfit, to celebrate her African heritage.

Next, her fairy Godmother asks June what her 2nd wish is, and she says that the second wish is to live in Los Angeles, California because a lot of movie stars live there. In fact, one of her favorite stars lives in Los Angeles, California, which is where Hollywood is. In addition, her cousin, Rashard lives there.

Then, June's fairy Godmother asks June what her 3rd wish is and tells her to think really hard about the last thing that she wants. June says that she does not need a third wish. If her name can be changed to Zarielle in time for the family reunion on Juneteenth (which is June 19th) and if they could move to Los Angeles, California, that would make her very happy. June's fairy Godmother tells her that her wishes will be granted, and June thanks her.

The next morning when June walks into the kitchen for breakfast, her dad says good morning little Zarielle. Then June's mom comes in and says, eat your pancakes Zarielle so that you won't be late for school. June thought to herself – this is so cool, my fairy Godmother said that my name would be changed, and the wish has been granted. It's like I was never named June. Then, June, who was now little Zarielle exclaimed: "I just love being named after you mommy because Zarielle is the most beautiful name in the world." Little Zarielle's mom laughed and said: "That's great, but we must hurry so that you're not late for school."

When she got to school, all of June's friends called her Zarielle and when her teacher, Ms. Green, called the roll to see who was here, she called out: Zarielle Jones. When she returned her test, the name Zarielle Jones was on the paper. June, who was now little Zarielle thought that this was the best day of her life!

Little Zarielle

When little Zarielle got home from school, her father had an important announcement to make during dinner. His job was transferring him to the Los Angeles office location, and they would be moving there next week. He explained to Zarielle why it had to be done right away and that he was sorry that she would have to go to a new school and leave her friends. Little Zarielle told her dad that it was okay, since there were only a few weeks left in the school year. Besides, she could have Zoom play dates and have Facetime with her best friend Jordan, and other friends. And also, that she would make new friends in Los Angeles. Little Zarielle also told her dad that she was excited because she always wanted to live in Los Angeles.

We are moving
to Los Angeles

When little Zarielle (who used to be named June) went to bed that night, she was so excited that she could barely sleep. Her fairy Godmother had granted both of her wishes: to move to Los Angeles and to be named Zarielle after her mother. This was her special Juneteenth name. As she fell asleep, little Zarielle thought of the rhyme: "I have a special Juneteenth NAME! It will bring me great FAME!"

The next week little Zarielle and her parents moved to Los Angeles. It was even better than she had imagined. Little Zarielle went and stood on the Hollywood walk of fame and went to Hollywood Elementary School, where she made new friends, many of them were child tv and movie stars. Little Zarielle loved her new life and it was all because her fairy Godmother had granted her two wishes. Zarielle's cousin, Rashard, also went to Hollywood Elementary School.

HOLLYWOOD ELEMENTARY SCHOOL

The weeks went by fast, and Little Zarielle was excited because it was almost time for their family reunion, that would be on Juneteenth Day, which was June 19. Little Zarielle had learned in school that Juneteenth was a combination of the words: June and Nineteen. Her family would travel back to Galveston, Texas, for the first time, since they had moved to Los Angeles, to attend the family reunion. Little Zarielle was going to enter the Little Miss Juneteenth Contest. She was thrilled because she had a special Juneteenth name and thought of the rhyme: I have a special Juneteenth NAME! It will bring me great FAME!

Little Zarielle (who used to be named June), and her mom were packing for their trip back to Galveston for their Juneteenth family reunion. While packing, little Zarielle's grandmother called them, and her mother put them on Facetime on her I. phone, so that little Zarielle could also see and talk to her grandmother. They began to talk about the night that little Zarielle was born. "Remember, when you were going to name her June at first and then decided to name her little Zarielle after yourself" said little Zarielle's grandmother. Little Zarielle's mother said: "Yes, I remember that night very well. It was 11:45 pm, when little Zarielle was born, and it was Juneteenth Eve." Juneteenth Eve is June 18th. "Right, and we could hear loud fireworks outside the hospital, because there was a big celebration and people were counting down to Juneteenth (June 19th), which was at 12:00 midnight" said little Zarielle's grandmother. "Oh what a glorious night that was." They said their goodbyes, ended the conversation and continued packing.

Later that evening, after the conversation with her grandmother, little Zarielle thought about how her name used to be June and that she had asked her fairy Godmother, who looked like an African Queen to grant her a wish and change her name to Zarielle, which was her mother's name. No one seemed to remember when her name was June. It was like little Zarielle had never been named June at all. Little Zarielle knew that her birthday was on June 18th, but she had never heard the day described as Juneteenth Eve. She knew that her family always had a big family reunion on Juneteenth Day, and she really liked that because she always got a lot of awesome birthday presents at the reunion. But little Zarielle did not know why they celebrated Juneteenth. The next day in school, little Zarielle asked her teacher, Ms. Garcia, if she could tell the class all about Juneteenth, which would be next week, after the school year ended.

"Why do we celebrate Juneteenth?"

Ms. Garcia said that first they must learn a rap: We're learning valuable history facts! Greatness is what this attracts!

Juneteenth, Take the word
We Love School!

Next, Ms. Garcia said that she would be happy to teach the class about Juneteenth and was glad that Zarielle had asked, because that was their lesson for the day and was already in her lesson plans. First, she explained the events leading up to Juneteenth.

Our country, the United States, gained its freedom from British rule, on July 4, 1776. However, not everyone was free. African people were stolen from their homeland, Africa and brought to the United States in ships. They became slaves, which means that they were the property of other people.   They were owned by other people – how unfair – for people to be owned by other people. Africans who lived in the United States were not treated fairly. Many worked on farms and picked cotton but did not get paid for their work.

African people who were slaves could not live where they wanted to live. They could not eat what they wanted to eat – they were given the left-over food and the food that their owners did not want to eat. They could not play what they wanted to play. The little slave children did not go to school – they worked in the fields or in their owners' houses. Most slaves did not know how to read or write because it was against the law for slaves to go to school and learn. In addition, it was illegal for other people to teach slaves how to read and write. Families, many times were separated. Children were often sold to other families. Slavery was a very bad thing.

NEGRO
PERSONS
FOR SALE

Not everyone in America liked slavery and thought that it was wrong. Some states in the northern part of our country said that slavery was illegal and stopped having slaves. Africans in those states were not slaves and were free. There was a former slave named Frederick Douglass who gave speeches about how bad slavery was. He was an abolitionist, which is someone who worked to put an end to slavery in the United States. Frederick Douglass had been born a slave but gained his freedom. Many in the United States celebrated Independence Day on July 4th because it was the date that Americans were freed from British rule. In one of his speeches, Frederick Douglass asked: "What to the American slave is your Fourth of July?" Mr. Douglass understood that people who were not free could not celebrate freedom.

African people did not like being slaves and they wanted to be free. There was a lady named Harriet Tubman. She had been a slave, but escaped and became a free person. But she wanted other slaves to be free, so she made many trips to the homes of slave owners and helped other slaves to escape to freedom. Harriet Tubman was very brave because helping slaves escape was very dangerous. If escaped slaves were caught, they were punished and beaten. Many wanted to stop Harriet Tubman because they did not want her to help other slaves to escape. Because of her brave acts, there was a reward for her capture and many people wanted to put her in jail. Harriet Tubman, who was known as Moses, was a hero.

FREEDOM

President Abraham Lincoln was elected in 1860, and he thought that slavery was wrong. Some in the southern part of our country thought that slavery was not wrong. On April 12, 1861, there was a Civil War that began between the Southern States and the Northern States in our country. This became a war to end slavery. During the war, on January 1, 1863, President Abraham Lincoln, sent out an order named the Emancipation Proclamation, which stated that all enslaved people in remaining states (who still had slaves) in the South were "forever free."

Even though slaves were free, and slavery had become illegal, in the state of Texas it was kept a secret from the slaves. The slaves were not told the truth about being free and they thought that they were still slaves. So, they continued to work for their masters. They did not have I. phones, Facebook, Tik-Tok, Instagram, Youtube, or the internet back in those times.

We're learning valuable history facts! Greatness is what this attracts!

RAP

The northern states won the Civil war on April 9, 1865. Then, on June 19, 1865, a General named Gordon Granger arrived in Galveston, Texas to announce to the slaves that they were free – it was no longer a secret. He made this declaration from a balcony. It took over 2 and ½ years for the slaves in Galveston, Texas to learn that they were free. (As President Lincoln had signed the Emancipation Proclamation confirming this on January 1, 1863). Once the announcement was made, the slaves started singing, dancing and hugging each other because they were so happy. June 19 became Independence Day for the former slaves. It was also known as Jubilee Day.

Wow thought little Zarielle. She thanked her teacher for helping her to learn all about Juneteenth Day. Little Zarielle thought: The family reunion that they have every year on Juneteenth Day, which is June 19th, is not just to give her birthday presents, but it is also to celebrate the end of slavery, which was a bad thing, in the United States.

Juneteenth is very important

Later, when she got home after school, little Zarielle told her parents what she had learned about Juneteenth. They were proud of her and told her that is why the street in downtown Galveston, Texas, is named after her great- great-great Grandmother Minnie Jones. She had been a slave and was there when General Gordon Granger made the announcement that the slaves were free on June 19th, 1865. She also said that in the future, there would be a great-great-great granddaughter whose favorite color was red, as red symbolizes the blood shed in the fight for freedom and the common heritage of Africans. Grandmother Jones said that child should be named "June." Little Zarielle thought to herself, that her favorite color was red, and she remembered that her name had been June before she asked her fairy Godmother for a wish to change her name to little Zarielle. That night, as she fell asleep, little Zarielle began to wonder if it was a good thing to ask her fairy Godmother for the wish to change her name.

Little Zarielle wanted to learn more about what happened after the slaves were free. The next morning, during breakfast, her father explained to her that even though the newly freed slaves were very happy to have their freedom, they still were not treated fairly and had to struggle. But they did not give up. He first told little Zarielle about an African American woman named Maggie L. Walker. Mrs. Walker's mother, Elizabeth Draper, had been a slave and so Mrs. Walker knew how hard it was for former slaves to survive. Mrs. Walker was born in Richmond, Virginia in 1864 and was well-known for being the first Black woman to establish and become the president of a bank in the United States. The name of the bank was the Saint Luke Penny Savings Bank, and it was located in Richmond, Virginia. Mrs. Walker, who had also been a teacher, served as president of the Saint Luke Penny Savings Bank from 1903 to 1929. Maggie L. Walker was a very smart and courageous woman, and even though freed slaves were not treated fairly, Mrs. Walker did not give up.

Bank President

Next, Zarielle's father told her about another great African American leader. In later years the sons and daughters of the former slaves started a Civil Rights movement and fought hard for the right to vote, to have jobs, and to go to schools where they would receive an equal education. There was a great preacher named Martin Luther King, Jr. who worked very hard in the Civil Rights movement and gave a great speech, entitled: "I Have a Dream."

Little Zarielle's mother continued the fascinating history in rich detail. In 1975, an African American male named Arthur Ashe, who was born in 1943 in Richmond, Virginia achieved a great accomplishment. He became the first Black man to win the Wimbledon men's single title and is currently the only Black man to win the Wimbledon men's title. In addition, Mr. Ashe was the only African American man to win the US Open title and the Austrian Open Title.

Then, Zarielle's mom told her about another great African American male. The African American people worked hard, went to school and they learned a lot. They never forgot how important Juneteenth was and it was always a joyous time for them to celebrate every year. Then, in 2008, Barack Obama was elected as the first African American president in the United States and another big celebration occurred.

Little Zarielle was very proud to learn that the first Juneteenth celebrations were held in Galveston, Texas, which is where she is from. Little Zarielle began to wonder if she had made the right choice when she asked her fairy Godmother if her family could live in Los Angeles, California. She had made many new friends in California. Now, that she had learned the history about where she was born, in Galveston Texas, she was so excited and wished that she still lived there and that her family had not moved to California.

Amarillo
Lubbock
Red River
Fort Worth
Dalles
Midland
Odessa
TEXAS
Waco
Austin
Houston
San Antonio
Calves
Laredo
Corpus Christi
Big Bend National Park
Rio Grande
Eromeville
& Padie Island
Culf Mex

While on the plane trip to Galveston, Texas for their Juneteenth Family Reunion, which would also be a birthday celebration for little Zarielle, her parents explained to her that on June 17, 2021, President Joe Biden (who was the vice-president when Barack Obama was the president) signed a bill making June 19th (Juneteenth) an official federal holiday in the United States.

Also, at the signing, was Kamala Harris, who is the first female vice president, first Black American and the first South Asian American vice president in the United States. In addition, in 2024, Mrs. Harris became the first Black American and the first South Asian American female presidential candidate in the United States.

Little Zarielle and her family arrived back in Galveston, Texas on June 17, which was the same date that President Joe Biden had signed the bill to make Juneteenth a federal holiday in 2021. Zarielle was happy to see her family, which included her cousins, grandparents and lots of uncles and aunts. Zarielle was most happy to see her best friend, Jordan. They had kept in contact and facetimed with each other a few times a week after Little Zarielle moved to Los Angeles.

Little Zarielle told Jordan that she was going to enter the Little Miss Juneteenth contest and Jordan thought that was a wonderful idea. That night when little Zarielle went to bed, in her previous bedroom, which was now in her aunt's house, she asked her fairy Godmother if she could have a third wish. Little Zarielle's fairy Godmother, who looked like an African Queen appeared and asked little Zarielle what she wanted for her third wish. Her first wish was to have her name changed from June to little Zarielle because she wanted to be named after her mother. Her second wish was to move from Galveston, Texas to Los Angeles, California. Little Zarielle told her fairy Godmother that her third wish was to have the first two wishes reversed. After learning the history of Juneteenth and what it meant, she was very proud of the name "June," which was the name that her mother had originally chosen for her. Her mother's name, Zarielle, was beautiful, but it was not the name that her mother had given her when she was born. While learning the history of Juneteenth, she was also very proud to learn that the slaves in Galveston, Texas which included many of her relatives, including her great-great-great grandmother, Minnie Jones (who the main street in Galveston was named after) were very brave people. In addition, Texas was the first state in the United States to declare Juneteenth a holiday. While Los Angeles was cool and she had some cousins that were there, she wanted to move back to Galveston, Texas. Little Zarielle's fairy Godmother told her that she was sorry, but the wishes could not be reversed once they were granted.

The next day is June 18th, and it is little Zarielle's birthday. But to Little Zarielle it is also Juneteenth Eve. Little Zarielle thinks about the story her grandmother and mother told her about the night that she was born, about there being lots of fireworks outside the hospital because there was a big countdown to Juneteenth, at midnight. Little Zarielle played with her best friend Jordan, ate some birthday cake and opened some of her birthday presents. She would get a lot more presents at the Jones Juneteenth Family reunion the next day, Juneteenth, which is June 19th. Little Zarielle began to write an essay for the Little Miss Juneteenth contest about what Juneteenth meant to her. An essay is a short piece of writing about a particular subject.

Juneteenth

Juneteenth is finally here, and it is time for the annual Jones Juneteenth family reunion. They are having a big barbecue in Jones City Park (which is named after Zarielle's family) in the center of the town, which is located on the street named after little Zarielle's great-great-great grandmother, Minnie Jones. Little Zarielle is so happy to see her family. In celebration of Juneteenth, they eat a lot of red foods and have red strawberry soda. There is a big red velvet birthday cake for Zarielle. There's lots of barbecue and hot dogs for everyone. Since little Zarielle's best friend Jordan is like family, she is there. Little Zarielle's cousin, Rashard is there also.

JONES Juneteenth REUNION
JON

It is now time for the Little Miss Juneteenth contest to begin. The winner of the contest will be the child who has written the best essay about what Juneteenth means to her. It is now little Zarielle's turn to go to the stage and read her essay. Little Zarielle announces that the title of her essay is: "My Special Juneteenth Name."

"This is a special story about a little girl who was born on Juneteenth Eve, which is June 18th. Her name is June, and she lives in Galveston, Texas with her mom and dad. One day, she asks her fairy Godmother to grant her two wishes. One wish is to be named after her mother, whom she adores and thinks has the most beautiful name ever. The little girl says that she would like to have her mother's name when they attend the Jones Juneteenth family reunion. It will be her special Juneteenth name. She even makes up a rhyme: "I have a special Juneteenth name. It will bring me great fame." The other wish is to move from Galveston, Texas to Los Angeles, California because her cousin Rashard and lots of movie stars live there. Her two wishes are granted and the next day everyone calls her by her new name and her dad announces that his job is transferring him to Los Angeles. Even though the little girl will miss her best friend, Jordan, very much, she is excited about going to school with her cousin, Rashard and the new friends that she will make in California.

Zarielle continues reading her essay. Every year, her family has a Jones Juneteenth family reunion on Juneteenth Day in the city and state where they are from, Galveston, Texas. While preparing for the family reunion, the little girl learns that on the night that she was born in Galveston, Texas, there were fireworks outside the hospital because people were counting down to midnight, which would be Juneteenth.

The crowd is very engaged in little Zarielle's essay and listens carefully as she continues reading it. The girl also learns that her mother wanted her first name to be June and her middle name to be Teenth and so her full name would be June Teenth Jones. Then the little girl learned about the history of Juneteenth and why it was so important, it was a celebration of the end of slavery, which was a very bad thing (African Americans were not treated fairly) in the United States.

Little Juneteenth

The little girl also learns that her great-great-great grandmother, who had been a slave and was there when General Gordon Granger made the announcement that the slaves were free was named Minnie Jones and the main street in Galveston was named after her. Her great-great-great grandmother helped to select her very name – she could look into the future and said that the grandchild whose favorite color was red should be named June. Then, the young child learned that Galveston, Texas was the first place to celebrate the Juneteenth holiday. After learning this amazing history, the child was very proud of her heritage and wanted to have her two wishes reversed. Knowledge is power and learning one's true history is the most powerful tool in the world. The little child learned that her special Juneteenth name was not the name that she asked her fairy Godmother to change, which was Zarielle. Her special Juneteenth name was the name that her parents had given her at birth: Juneteenth Jones. Then she announced that the little child was herself.

Everyone stood up and clapped and said that it was by far the best essay that they had heard in all of the years that they had a Little Miss Juneteenth contest. When it was time for them to announce the winner of the contest, they called all the contestants to the stage and said that the winner of the contest was Juneteenth Jones and placed a crown on her head and a sash around her with the words: Little Miss Juneteenth. The little girl was so happy and excited and asked: "What did you say my name is?" Her parents were in the front row laughing and said, it's Juneteenth Jones, like it has always been. Little Juneteenth (who had wished to be named little Zarielle), was now the happiest girl in the whole world and said the cheer: "I have a special Juneteenth name.
It will bring me great fame."

Then, little Juneteenth (who wished she had a different name before she learned a valuable history lesson), asked her parents if they could stay in Galveston, Texas for the rest of the summer. They informed her that since they lived in Galveston, Texas, they could stay there all year round and started to laugh. But we just came from California, Juneteenth said. Her parents reminded her that it was a work trip to a conference that her father was attending. While there, for a few weeks, Juneteenth got to go to school with her cousin Rashard. And it got even better, Rashard would be there to visit with Juneteenth for the entire summer. Wow – this was really turning out to be the best day in Juneteenth's life.

Later, in the day, Juneteenth saw one of her aunts and realized that she was her fairy Godmother and thanked her for reversing her 2 wishes. Her aunt explained to her that it was not her doing. The only way for the 2 wishes to be reversed was for little Juneteenth to learn her family history, the history of Juneteenth and why she was named Juneteenth, then she had to make a public announcement about what she had learned. She did this when she read her essay entitled: "My Special Juneteenth Name."

As Juneteenth played with her cousin Rashard, and best friend Jordan, she thought about how blessed she was to learn her true history. Juneteenth is a true celebration for the entire United States. Juneteenth decided to have another slice of the red velvet cake for this especially joyous occasion. She and her friends repeated the cheer together: "I have a special Juneteenth name. It will bring me great fame!"

Meet the Author

Darlene Green is an award-winning storyteller and puppeteer and has been the president of D. Green Storytelling since 2011. On June 18, 2024, the organization was excited to present the first annual Juneteenth Storytelling and Puppet Show to the community. The citizens of Virginia Beach funded the event through a grant from the City of Virginia Beach Arts & Humanities Commission.

Ms. Green also serves in a Gold Medal Preschool Program and has enjoyed teaching children in Virginia for 25 years. She graduated from San Francisco State University and earned her teaching certification from Norfolk State University.

In the fall of 2018, Ms. Green received the President's Lifetime Achievement Award for her dedication to serving the community. She has volunteered for more than 4,000 hours over 20 years at local libraries where she performs educational skits and hosts book readings for children.

Ms. Green, a lifelong Catholic, is a member of the Basilica of St. Mary of the Immaculate Conception Church in Norfolk, Virginia and was inspired to feature youth from her church in her first book, Imani and the 3 Rosaries.

Her church ministries have included Lector, Eucharistic Minister, and a Rosary Leader. She Looks forward to writing more books.